Somatic Therapy Guide for Healing Trauma

Little Known Techniques and Exercises to Relief Stress, PTSD, Enhance Body-Mind Connection, Emotional Regulation and Resilience for Adult

Thomas Levine

Copyright © 2023 by Thomas Levine

All rights reserved.

This book is written as a source of information only. The information contained in this book is provided in good faith and is believed to be accurate and reliable as of the date of publication. The author does not assume any responsibility for any errors or omissions that may appear.

Table of Content

INTRODUCTION

Somatic therapy, a holistic approach to mental health and well-being, delves into the intricate connection between the mind and body. Unlike traditional therapeutic methods that primarily focus on verbal communication, somatic therapy recognizes bodily experiences and sensations' profound impact on one's emotional and psychological state. Rooted in the belief that the body holds the key to unlocking deep-seated traumas and fostering healing, this therapeutic modality has gained prominence for its integrative and comprehensive approach to addressing mental health challenges.

At its core, somatic therapy operates on the premise that the body and mind are interconnected, forming an intricate system where emotional, physical, and psychological elements coalesce. Developed as an alternative to conventional talk therapies, somatic therapy acknowledges the significance of bodily experiences in shaping one's emotional responses, stress levels, and overall mental well-being. This therapeutic approach strives to bridge the gap between an individual's conscious and unconscious aspects, promoting self-awareness and facilitating the release of stored tension and trauma within the body.

Central to bodily therapy is the understanding that our bodies retain memories of past experiences, particularly those associated with trauma or stress. These memories can manifest as physical sensations, chronic pain, or emotional disturbances, creating barriers to a person's overall sense of harmony and balance. Somatic therapists employ various techniques to guide individuals in reconnecting with their bodily sensations, helping them explore and process unresolved emotions and ultimately fostering a more integrated and balanced state of being.

One of the key principles of somatic therapy is the emphasis on mindfulness and present-moment awareness. Practitioners guide clients to tune into their bodily sensations, encouraging a non-judgmental observation of thoughts and feelings as they arise. By cultivating this awareness, individuals can better understand the intricate interplay between their physical sensations and emotional responses. This heightened awareness becomes a powerful tool for navigating life's challenges, fostering resilience, and promoting overall well-being.

Somatic therapy encompasses diverse modalities, each tailored to address specific aspects of the mind-body connection. Body-oriented techniques such as breathwork, movement, and touch are integral components of somatic therapy, facilitating the release of tension and promoting a sense of embodiment. Through these practices, individuals can explore and express their emotions, unearthing hidden layers of experience that may influence their mental health.

Embarking on a somatic therapy journey involves exploring bodily sensations and movements guided by a skilled and empathetic therapist. This collaborative process encourages clients to become attuned to their bodily experiences, recognizing the significance of subtle cues and signals. The therapist acts as a supportive guide, facilitating the integration of emotional and physical aspects of the self and helping clients develop tools for self-regulation and stress management.

Somatic therapy is not limited to addressing specific mental health disorders; instead, it offers a versatile framework that can benefit individuals dealing with a range of challenges, from stress and anxiety to more complex trauma-related issues. This inclusive approach recognizes the uniqueness of each person's experience and tailors interventions to suit individual needs. By acknowledging the inherent wisdom of the body and its role in the therapeutic process, somatic therapy provides a profound avenue for self-discovery and healing.

In the following chapters, we will delve deeper into somatic therapy's core principles and techniques, exploring how this innovative approach contributes to the mental health field and complements traditional therapeutic modalities. We will examine the role of the body in storing and processing emotions, the importance of somatic awareness in trauma recovery, and the diverse range of somatic techniques employed by therapists to facilitate healing and personal growth. Through this exploration, we aim to shed light on the transformative potential of somatic therapy in enhancing overall well-being and promoting a harmonious integration of mind and body.

CHAPTER ONE

UNDERSTANDING SOMATIC THERAPY

"Somatic" refers to body-related; "somatic therapy" seeks to release trauma held inside our bodies. Somatic therapy involves using physical techniques that have a direct impact on the body to treat mental health issues. Another name for it is somatic experiencing (SE) therapy, which Peter Levine created during his investigation into mind-body connections.

Body awareness combined with traditional counselling is how somatic psychology and SE work to treat mental health disorders and help people overcome trauma.

This can also involve counselling techniques like eye movement desensitization and reprocessing (EMDR), which makes use of eye movements to help people with traumatized minds regain their mental wellness. Most somatic experience therapists hold the view that any emotional trauma can result in Autonomic Nerve System (ANS) instability.

To fend against dangers, human systems have evolved to thicken blood, direct blood away from extremities and towards key organs, and increase respiration and heart rate. In the past, these modifications could have helped humans avoid physical harm, but they might not necessarily be helpful in the face of contemporary pressures. Furthermore, persistent stresses have the potential to trap our bodies in a perpetual state of trauma, tension, or pent-up emotions. These alterations in our autonomic nerve systems might also result from trauma reactions.

You could face the psychological and physical repercussions of a traumatic encounter or event. Headaches, nausea, pains in the muscles, and other symptoms that are felt throughout the body can all be signs of trauma.

Those with post-traumatic stress disorder (PTSD) and trauma can both benefit from somatic treatment. Additional advantages of somatic treatment consist of:

- Improved control over emotions
- Assistance for persistent pain
- A greater awareness of oneself

- Handling symptoms of mental illnesses such as sadness and anxiety
- Instruments for managing and processing feelings and encounters

Numerous individuals can benefit from somatic therapy. It can benefit trauma survivors, sufferers of anxiety and depression, persons with long-term medical conditions, athletes, entertainers, and anybody else who might have suppressed their stress and feelings.

Introduction To Somatic Therapy

Somatic therapy, a body-focused branch of psychology, is the foundation of somatic treatment. Somatic therapy functions by addressing the ongoing feedback loop that exists between the body and the mind. Typical psychotherapy (talk therapy) is not the same as somatic therapy. In standard psychotherapy, the therapist works with the patient's thinking. The body serves as the cornerstone for healing in somatic therapy.

Somatic therapists hold that a person's unpleasant emotions, including those felt following a traumatic incident, might remain trapped inside the body. These unpleasant feelings might develop into psychiatric diseases or physical issues like neck or back pain if they are not let go of promptly. Those who have been identified as having post-traumatic stress disorder (PTSD) frequently have severe discomfort.

Somatic therapists employ mind-body methods to help you let go of the stress that is negatively impacting your physical and mental health. These methods could include dance, meditation, breathing exercises, and other physical movements. Somatic therapy practitioners believe that the mind and body are inextricably intertwined. Additionally, they think that trauma and other persistently bad feelings can become lodged in our bodies and have an even greater harmful impact on our mental health. The goal of somatic therapy is to promote cellular healing.

The nervous system may become locked into survival mode following a stressful incident. Constant production of stress hormones, including cortisol, raises blood pressure and blood sugar, compromising immunological function. Physical symptoms appear when the body is constantly under this much stress.

Furthermore, negative events can give rise to deeply ingrained beliefs hidden from our conscious awareness. These could include unfavourable or detrimental ideas like "I'm a bad person" or "I'll never succeed." Such unfavourable emotions are not alone stored in the body; they also surface frequently. Trauma survivors face reactivation of their symptoms when they encounter fresh, stressful situations. This can make them feel traumatized over and over. Somatic experience is predicated on the idea that PTSD symptoms are a manifestation of stress activation.

A detailed account of the traumatic incident is typically not necessary for somatic experiencing, in contrast to exposure therapy, which is a popular type of treatment for PTSD. Instead, the client considers stressful events from the past and learns how to reduce arousal using different body awareness exercises and painful recollections.

A somatic psychotherapist can assist in the physical discharge of trauma or bad emotions through a variety of treatments. Here are a few of the more well-known ones:

- **Body Awareness:** One of the first stages towards learning to relieve physical tension in the body is this method. In addition to learning how to calm thoughts and feelings, the client also learns to detect and identify body tense spots.
- **Grounding:** This is to establish a strong connection between your body and the earth's surface. Sensing your body, feeling your feet on the ground, and lowering your stress level are all part of grounding.

- **Pendulation:** Using this method, a therapist leads you from a calm condition to one that resembles a traumatic event. You can let go of the stored-up energy by repeating this multiple times. As the energy is released, you can experience uneasiness or nervousness. You'll be led back to a calm state each time. You will eventually have the ability to unwind by yourself.

- **Titration:** The therapist walks you through a painful recollection using this method. You will be asked to note any physical changes as you explain the recollection. The therapist will assist you in addressing any bodily sensations as they arise.

- **Sequencing:** This feature is being very aware of the sequence in which your body releases tension-causing sensations. For example, you may experience a constriction in your throat followed by a constriction in your chest. Subsequently, as the pressure leaves your body, you can experience quivering.

- **Resourcing:** It entails thinking back on the things in your life—like your relationships, your strongest traits, or even a special vacation destination—that gives you a sense of security. It might consist of anything that soothes you. The positive emotions and experiences connected to your resources then return to you, providing a psychological anchoring.

Any deep-seated, internally stored negative emotion can be treated with somatic therapy. Although trauma is usually the cause of this, therapy can also benefit those who struggle with:

• Sorrow

• Fury

• Anxiety

• Depression

• Trust issues

• Affection

• Insecurity

Types of Somatic Therapy

The following list includes some of the most popular types of somatic therapy:

- **Somatic Experiencing:**

This type of therapy addresses the body's reactions to trauma. Some somatic therapists may ask you to talk about your traumatic experiences, while others may only ask you to describe the physical sensations you experienced during the traumatic event. You may also be asked to move your body in a way that elicits negative feelings; in either case, the therapist will teach you how to release the built-up energy and gradually eliminate the triggers safely.

- **EMDR:**

In the process of EMDR, the patient recalls traumatic events in brief bursts while focusing on an external stimulus. Common focal points include sideways eye movements, hand tapping, or listening to a specific sound.

- **Hakomi:**

Mindfulness, or the capacity to observe the current moment without passing judgment, is the foundation of this kind of somatic therapy. The practitioner helps the client recognize physical cues indicating unconscious beliefs after creating a compassionate acceptance environment. The individual interacts with the therapist to safely discharge unconscious material, gaining access to it quickly.

- **Sensorimotor Psychotherapy:**

In addition to approaches from the Hakomi method, psychomotor psychotherapy incorporates concepts from neuroscience, somatic therapy, attachment theory, and psychotherapy. Through safe reenactment of a traumatic event, the client is assisted in completing any unfinished acts (such as not being able to defend themselves from an attacker) from the original occurrence. The goal of doing this is to have a sense of closure and fulfilment.

Neurosomatic Treatment:

Neurosomatic treatment benefits patients with symptoms close to the actual part of the mind and body connection. NST finds the hidden causes of physical discomfort and stress in the skeletal, nervous, and soft tissues. This method primarily uses massage, posture correction exercises, and imbalance-correcting exercises.

History and Evolution

Wilhelm Reich, the originator of somatic psychotherapy, is credited with developing the idea and drawing a parallel between it and unicellular creatures. Psychiatrists Alexander Lowen and John Pierrakos developed Bioenergetics, building on Reich's core beliefs and drawing a parallel between the rhythm of this life force energy and that of a pendulum.

Although there have been many pioneers in the field of somatics, we will concentrate on people who were crucial in creating somatic psychotherapy, the foundation for the work of other well-known therapists you are likely familiar with.

Wilhelm Reich

Wilhelm Reich, a talented Austrian psychiatrist and psychologist, is where our story starts in the early 1900s. Reich has been credited as the pioneer of somatic psychology. Born in 1897, Reich became very interested in psychoanalysis and Sigmund Freud's writings, which greatly influenced his early professional life.

Reich formulated his distinct method in the 1920s and dubbed it "character analysis." In 1933, he also wrote a book with the same title. He thought that psychological problems originated in the mind and showed themselves physically and that human impulses are inherently positive. Reich postulated that emotions and tensions were retained in the body's tissues and preserved as muscular structures. This he named Armoring as well. Since infancy, you have been observing and evaluating your surroundings, including your parents, siblings, friends, and teachers. Your body has evolved to protect you. Your regular posture, attitude, and mannerisms form a self-protective armour that you wear. He felt that people may undergo significant mental and emotional healing by identifying and discharging these physical tensions through bodywork, expressive movement, and deep breathing.

Through his research into the body's energetic systems and his work with patients, Reich developed the idea of "orgone energy." Orgone energy is a universal life force that permeates everything around us.

It is related to what other traditions have called prana or chi and affects our mental and physical health. He thought that a variety of psychological and physical illnesses could result from disturbances in the flow of orgone energy. Reich created a variety of healing methods to free trapped energy and re-establish orgone energy's natural flow. Reich felt that unresolved emotional problems might be released through the body through therapy, resulting in better well-being.

While some found Reich's theories intriguing, the scientific community viewed them with suspicion and scorn. His theories regarding orgone energy and the effectiveness of the orgone accumulator were rejected as pseudoscientific and devoid of factual support. Reich had a string of disagreements with the scientific and medical establishment, which resulted in his detention and the destruction of his study records.

Though his work has been controversial, Reich has left a lasting influence on somatic psychotherapy. He cleared the path for further advancements in body-oriented therapies, like bioenergetics and sensorimotor psychotherapy, by emphasizing the mind-body link, recognizing the body's intelligence during recovery, and using the body to address emotional problems.

Alexander Lowen

Lowen addressed the relationship between the mind and the body in healing by fusing body-oriented approaches with psychotherapy, drawing on his training in health and his readings of Wilhelm Reich's work. According to Lowen, psychological problems and emotional conflicts are not just confined to the mind but are also engrained in the body. He promoted an integrated approach to therapy and stressed the need to comprehend the body's function in mental well-being. Lowen made significant contributions, including the idea of "bioenergetics." According to his theory, the body is a complex energetic system, and the tension and energy flow in its muscles reflect psychological processes and emotions.

Building on Wilhelm Reich's work with body armour, he thought that breathing rhythms, muscular rigidity, and postural habits are all ways that the body expresses emotional and energetic patterns. Lowen sought to facilitate psychological well-being by releasing emotional barriers through bodywork.

To assist people in re-establishing a connection with their bodies and letting go of pent-up stress and trauma, Lowen created a variety of exercises and treatments. Some strategies include breathwork, movement exercises, body-centred awareness practices, and grounding exercises. Understanding the body's wisdom and ability to express and release emotions was fundamental to Lowen's method. He felt that people may achieve significant emotional healing and physical symptom relief by accessing and releasing trapped energy in their bodies. In addition, Lowen's research highlighted the significance of nonverbal cues and body language in revealing a person's emotional state. He distinguished between various body types and posture patterns linked to character structures, which are thought to represent emotional and psychological patterns. He integrated this insight into his therapy method since he felt that the body frequently conveyed more about a person's genuine feelings and ideas than words alone.

Alexander Lowen popularized and developed the area of somatic psychotherapy through his writings, which include "Bioenergetics" and "The Betrayal of the Body," as well as his workshops and lectures. Numerous therapists and people looking to establish a stronger bond between their physical and mental health have been impacted by his work.

Pierre Janet

Understanding and treating psychiatric problems, particularly those associated with trauma and dissociation, was the focus of Janet's work. He had a particular interest in researching how traumatic events affected a person's mental state as well as how these incidents showed up in their consciousness and behaviours.

One of Janet's most influential theories was "dissociation," which is now a common notion and conversation topic when discussing trauma and its physiological impacts. As the pioneer in dissociation research, Janet demonstrated how traumatic memories might manifest as affect states, sensory experiences, and behavioural reenactments. He noticed that people who had gone through trauma frequently reported a divide or detachment in their consciousness. Feelings of detachment from reality, forgetfulness, and depersonalization were among the symptoms of this dissociation. Janet would later create a thorough theory of dissociation. He thought that from a person's conscious consciousness, traumatic memories could become dissociated, resulting in the development of distinct psychological states or subpersonalities.

Janet's therapy aimed to comprehend and reconcile these separated aspects of the self. He felt people might repair and reconcile their broken sense of self by accessing and investigating the painful experiences connected to these subpersonalities. You may already be hearing parallels to some of the more well-known somatic techniques available today, such as Internal Family Systems and Somatic Experiencing.

Janet used various therapeutic methods to help in this process, such as dream interpretation, hypnosis, and what he called "psychological analysis." He was kind and sympathetic, giving his patients a secure and encouraging space to discover their inner selves. Janet was a key pioneer in the development of somatic psychotherapy because he understood the mind-body connection and the significance of the body in psychological illnesses. He realized that physical symptoms and sensations could sometimes be signs of trauma and dissociation in addition to mental ones. His understanding of the significant effects that traumatic events have on the human mind has influenced how we currently address and treat psychological trauma.

Eugene Gendlin

His research focused on "felt sense," a visceral understanding of a circumstance or problem. He held that a plethora of implicit wisdom and knowledge resides in our bodies, which can help us comprehend and resolve emotional conflicts and other obstacles in life.

Gendlin created the "focusing" technique to assist people in accessing and examining their felt sense. He suggested that by paying close attention to and exploring physical sensations and emotional experiences with empathy, one can access the implicit, preverbal information and wisdom that the body possesses. By paying close attention to the body and observing even the smallest physiological sensations, one can learn to focus and allow more profound understanding and meaning to emerge. Focusing is a technique that helps people access their inner wisdom and better understand their feelings, experiences, and circumstances in life. By fostering a closer bond between the mind, body, and emotions, focusing offers a route for self-awareness and personal development.

Beyond individual treatment, Gendlin's contributions impacted the creation of Focusing-Oriented treatment. Focusing is a fundamental element of this therapeutic technique, highlighting the value of experiential inquiry and body awareness in healing. Focusing-oriented therapy involves the therapist supporting the patient in developing a nonjudgmental and loving presence, exploring their sensations, paying attention to their body wisdom, and verbally expressing their experiences.

Numerous therapeutic methods, such as somatic psychotherapy, mindfulness-based approaches, cognitive-behavioural therapy, and psychodynamic therapy, have heavily incorporated Gendlin's work. Our knowledge of the mind-body link has grown because of his dedication to the body's inherent intellect and its coordination of felt sensations.

Theoretical Frameworks (Body-mind Connection)

The foundation of somatic therapy theory is the notion that events in an individual's life, especially traumatic ones, are stored in both the body and the brain. The mind-body or somatic connection is the relationship between your thoughts and emotions. This notion states that therapy focusing on the mind-body link might help a patient heal. "Feelings" implies a sense that is experienced physically. An individual's thoughts influence their feelings, and vice versa. According to a theory, a person's mind and body are affected when thinking negatively. The notion that the body and mind are interconnected creates a healing avenue for mental health conditions such as addiction, stress, anxiety, and trauma.

The body's capacity for self-healing, both physiologically and psychologically, is remarkable. The body attempts to keep you safe and communicates with the brain continuously to keep everything in balance. According to the polyvagal theory, the autonomic nervous system of mammals has evolved to adopt behavioural strategies such as survival and safety. The polyvagal hypothesis can be used in somatic experiences and practices in somatic therapy to aid in the physical and emotional discharge of trauma. In a safe and healthy approach, polyvagal-informed somatic therapy can assist an individual in working with their nervous system instead of against it.

Where in the Body Is Trauma Stored?

Research indicates that trauma is preserved in somatic memory and manifests as alterations in the physiologic stress response. People unblock their bodies from repressed emotions in a variety of ways. Some of these include:

- Recognizing and naming the feelings and emotions that are present is the first step towards releasing repressed emotions.
- Next, it's critical to discover strategies for overcoming these prior traumas, typically with a therapist's assistance.
- Intentional movement is the primary tool in somatic therapy to help the body release these pent-up feelings.
- Apart from therapy, isolating yourself, engaging in meaningful physical activity, walking outside, practising silence and mindfulness, and listening to music could be beneficial.

Physical Signs Indicating Trauma Release

Physical indications and symptoms of releasing tension and trauma include:

- Trembling
- Weeping
- Profuse sweating
- Variations in breathing
- Tension in the muscles
- Heart palpitating

- A person may experience feelings of freedom, lightness, and happiness when their body releases trauma.

Key Concepts and Principles

The paradigm known as SIBAM (Sensation, Imagery, Behavior, Affect, and Meaning) is used by somatic experience practitioners to assist clients in integrating their bodies in processing trauma. Most therapy typically employs "top-down" techniques, utilizing cognitive abilities to retrieve memories or traumas. On the other hand, somatic experiencing takes a "bottom-up" strategy, starting with physical experiences and returning to our thinking.

- **Sensation:** You might not be accustomed to resting with the bodily sensations flowing through you, or you might not have known how they related to your feelings. You will start by just observing your bodily sensations.

- **Imagery:** This framework section uses interactive or guided imagery, in which a practitioner walks you through envisioning a scene while you listen. In the latter, you and the practitioner have a continuous conversation in which you discuss any issues that arise while you are guided through this activity.

- **Behavior:** Levine's model includes a behaviour component where the therapist observes your behavioural responses, such as your posture or body language, even though you will be expressing your internal feelings for most of this therapy.

- **Affect:** It refers to how you communicate your feelings to the external environment through your tone, phrasing, and speed, among other things.

- **Meaning:** Lastly, this model section examines your perception of the therapy and the personal significance of what you have gone through.

The foundation of somatic therapy is that your body stores memories of the events in your life and your intellect. This all-encompassing approach to treatment focuses on talking about your issues and the physical experiences you have in your body.

CHAPTER TWO

THE BODY'S ROLE IN HEALING

It might take years for PTSD to go away in a person whom a lion pursued. Even though a similar survival mechanism is at work, a human's body does not go through the cycle like an animal's. The gazelle will gallop, skip, leap, play with other animals, jump in the water, or engage in other activities once it has reached a safe area. The trauma process is completed by the animal's instinctive discharge of all the energy produced by releasing stress hormones. Conversely, humans tend to freeze up. Shaking it off is not usually the end of running for our lives, either literally or figuratively. People's inability to "shake off" their terrible experiences is what leads directly to post-traumatic stress disorder.

Trauma-related stress is retained in our bodies because we freeze. We frequently cannot fully recover from trauma until we are freed from the physical prison of traumatic experiences, which keeps the memory of trauma intact in the very molecular structure of our being.

The idea that what happens to you stays with you underlies the way both your body and mind work. Additionally, somatic therapy holds that your body and mind retain all that occurs to you during your lifetime. The body serves as the foundation for healing in somatic therapy. This type of treatment allows patients to feel secure in their skin while investigating ideas, feelings, and memories. It also fosters an awareness of one's body sensations. Movement is frequently used in somatic psychotherapy to assist in balancing the autonomic nervous system and achieve a condition known as "biological completion," in which repressed arousal energy has been released and the system is back in equilibrium. Breathwork and "moving meditations," like tai chi, yoga, and qigong, can assist in activating the vagus nerve and alleviate physical symptoms of trauma, such as headaches and muscular soreness.

Somatic psychology incorporates current psychology, biology, and neuroscience findings with ancient mind-body practices. As new knowledge about the close and incredibly potent connections between the brain and body emerges, somatic psychotherapy expands, offering additional chances to promote the body's natural healing process—one little step at a time—repair from trauma.

Body-Centered Approach to Therapy

Experiential therapy, known as body-centred psychotherapy, is predicated on the notion that our bodies are repositories of knowledge and feelings. In other words, events and emotions are stored as bodily recollections. To help you access your feelings, body-centred psychotherapy looks for places where experiences could be inhibited. You can give your body a "voice" and gain insight into ingrained thinking, emotion, or behaviour patterns through movement, gesture, sound, and awareness of subtle sensations. Gaining awareness and knowledge via this process may assist you in creating a strong sense of inner knowing, lowering anxiety and sadness, making wise judgments, establishing boundaries in relationships, and feeling more secure and focused.

Western societies, such as ours, place a high value on knowledge acquisition, problem-solving skills, and the ability to justify or give reasons for our decisions. But occasionally, our emotional states and reason are incompatible. This internal division or dichotomy might cause us to feel overwhelmed and anxious. We may improve our understanding of who we are, increase our self-acceptance, and break bad habits by utilizing the body's knowledge.

Our ability to listen and our decision about responding will determine the advantages we can derive from what our bodies are trying to tell us. We may start living more physically and mentally healthy lives by focusing on our full selves, or what I refer to as our body brains, alongside our thinking brains. Certain bodily indicators may appear apparent, such as a rumbling stomach indicating hunger or yawning indicating weariness.

- But frequently, our bodies communicate with us in more intricate and unique ways than that:
- In treatment, we learn that a long-standing tendency of child abuse victims is to look down and away from authority people to divert their attention or vent their wrath.
- A mature woman understands that, like a kid waiting for terrible news, she holds her breath until her spouse finishes speaking.
- A guy who suffers from chronic pain discovers that years of protecting himself from criticism have made him anxious, worn out, and cautious around people.
- A bulimic young lady connects the dots, stating that she feels somewhat satisfied with the rawness in her throat, as though she had punished herself for being flawed.

Through body-centred psychotherapy, we may access memories, feelings, and beliefs that would otherwise be beyond our language and understanding. Body-centred psychotherapy might help you rediscover how your mind and body communicate.

How Trauma Manifests Physically

Fearful, hazardous, or startling situations that impact our bodily, mental, spiritual, or social well-being are known as traumatic events. Natural disasters, wars, terrorist attacks, mass shootings, severe diseases, automobile accidents, workplace accidents, rape, abuse, and other situations that impair our feeling of well-being are a few examples of traumatic occurrences.

Trauma has different effects on us. Over time, it can impact our behaviour, mental health, and capacity for function. It might trigger emotional reactions in the near term, including fear, disorientation, shock, isolation, and dissociation. In addition to causing physical symptoms like headaches, nausea, racing heartbeat, poor sleep quality, and an inclination to startle quickly, trauma can also place the body in a state of stress.

Trauma frequently shows itself both emotionally and physically. Frequent physical indicators of trauma include paleness, exhaustion, lethargy, difficulty concentrating, and a racing heartbeat. In such situations, the victim may have anxiety or panic attacks and find it difficult to handle things. Each of us responds to trauma differently, going through a spectrum of emotional and physical responses. Remember that there is no "right" or "wrong" way to feel, think, or behave, so stop criticizing yourself or other people for how you react; you are responding to abnormal occurrences normally.

Some of the typical signs of unresolved trauma are as follows:

- An unwillingness to lower one's guard and keen awareness.

- Inability to trust others and discomfort being vulnerable with them.

- Dissociation and a numbness that never goes away.

- Control problems are an excessive attempt to make up for feeling powerless during a painful event.

- Poor self-worth and a sense of unworthiness

- Anger management problems and emotional dysregulation.

- Elevated cortisol and blood pressure levels.

- Problems with sleep, such as nightmares and insomnia.

- Sweating, headaches, nausea, or digestive problems.

- Stomach pit or constriction in the chest.

- Somatic preoccupation: an intense fixation on somatic sensations combined with intense distress.

- Bodily recollections of the pressure, agony, taste, smell, and feelings of the traumatic event bring on physical flashbacks.

- Mental health disorders such as post-traumatic stress disorder (PTSD), depression, anxiety, and drug abuse disorders

Other physical manifestations of trauma include:

- Fatigue

- Becoming quickly alarmed.

- Inability to concentrate.

- Pounding heart rate.

- Anxiety and restlessness.

- Pains and aches.

- Tense muscles.

Neurobiology of Somatic Experiences

The scientific study of behaviour, cognition, brain mapping, and the nervous system's biology is collectively called neuroscience.

Together, the fields of biology and psychology from neuroscience. The nervous system is the source of human perception and thought. Therefore, the nervous system study must go beyond the biological structure covered by neurobiology and incorporate the mechanical analysis of the relationships between each biological component and human function, perception, thought, memory, and cognition.

The study of neuroscience includes an examination of the captain who guides the ship and its crew as well as the vessel that carries us. The study of the nerve system's cells and tissue is known as neurobiology. The brain, spine, neural circuits, and nerves that supply all parts of the body make up the nervous system. The study of neurobiology focuses on the physiology of each nervous system component and how they work together. Other scientific fields like gene control and molecular biology can be included in neurobiology. We shall now discuss the specifics of neurology in somatic experiences as, as we can see from the definitions of the terminology, neurobiology is a subfield of neurosciences.

The fields of neurosciences have made significant contributions to our understanding of the neurobiological underpinnings of the following changes in the brain that are useful for psychotherapy practice:

- Somatic symptoms and disorders

- Mirror neurons system and theory of mind (ToM)

- Memory of trauma

- Neurobiological correlates of human attachment

By integrating the body's experience with the brain's interpretation of social interactions, the environment, traumas, and medical events, neurology and somatic therapy have been collaborating to find and integrate contemporary integrative therapy models and methodologies.

Scientists, psychologists, and medical professionals are creating new hypotheses on how the body and brain interact to transmit and receive signals and information via contemporary technology, clinical study, and professional observation. Health professionals, therapists, and individuals can combine traditional knowledge with modern technologies to create effective, individualized therapies and treatment plans that sustain individual and collective health and well-being. This can be achieved using emerging evidence and new integrative thought models.

The study of cognitive neuroscience sheds light on the differences between the left and right brain's functions by examining how the brain's neural circuits create cognitive and psychological processes.

All the information about ourselves and our lives, including our name, date of birth, residence, likes and dislikes, language, profession, and other identifiers, is stored in the left brain and the ego centre. The left brain processes information quickly and efficiently because of its superior ability to recognize patterns. It also uses this ability to predict our subconscious reactions to events, including future thoughts, feelings, and behaviours based on prior experiences. The left brain informs us about the world and our role through critical thought, judgment, and analysis.

The right brain sees the larger context and imagines it abstractly, assessing nonverbal cues like tone of voice, body language, and facial expression to determine how much faith we should put in the security of the situation or whether dishonesty and danger are imminent. The right brain softens the left brain's extremely literal readings of communication, placing it in the appropriate context. Together, the brain's left and right hemispheres function as a complementary unit to provide our conscious mind with accurate views of our environment and a range of appropriate reactions from which to select.

When a person is injured in one hemisphere of the brain, their ability to think and respond appropriately is compromised.

While right brain injury can result in a lack of psychological or contextual speech interpretation, left brain damage frequently causes speech difficulty or loss. The brain's remarkable capacity to heal from stress involves rerouting or rebuilding damaged neuronal pathways—a process known as neuroplasticity. By improving the functionality of regularly utilized synaptic connections and eliminating the usage of seldom used pathways, the brain adapts through neuroplasticity to better handle information about our daily lives and reality more quickly and effectively. The brain's ability to adapt the information it absorbs or concentrates on, known as neuroplasticity, affects our automatic responses to daily situations. Many therapeutic models and medical interventions may be used to speed up the healing process from trauma, and recorded patient outcomes and scientific measures indicate that sound and music are among the most powerful tools for promoting patient recovery. Neurotransmitters at the end of blocked pathways cannot convert the electrical energy flowing through the damaged pathways into an appropriate chemical context when traumatic events occur in the brain or body, whether medical events or severe physical/emotional traumas. Consider this phenomenon as an earthquake-related blockage of a regularly functioning highway:

- The earthquake represents a traumatic experience.

- The rubble represents a disruption in brain pathways.

- The cars on the road represent electrical energy.

Role of Sensations and Body Awareness

All too frequently, the messages we are exposed to from society rob us of our authentic feelings, our experiences in the here and now, and our best selves. We become disoriented, estranged, and self-conscious as we try to negotiate this society of distraction. It's gotten much too simple to lose ourselves in our thoughts, whether past or future-related. This division and physical disconnection are largely why becoming more conscious of your body is crucial and frequently enlightening.

What is body awareness?

Having a conscious connection to one's body instead of the mind and body being as distinct entities is known as body awareness. We developed bodily awareness in tandem with crawling and walking when we were born, and we advanced like most people do, learning things like how high to climb stairs or how far to reach objects. In this environment, body awareness becomes second nature to adults because of everyday experiences, including perception and spatial awareness of our physical self.

How Somatic Therapy Affects Body Awareness

It encompasses far more than just our physical identities in this context. Body awareness is the understanding of our body and mind as one and our reactions or behaviour. Being mindful of one's body is helpful in treatment because our bodies retain memories and experiences from the past, which manifests itself in our posture, expressions, and body language. An unsettled stomach, migraines, hormone imbalances, and other medical disorders can be brought on by physical symptoms of trauma. Research has indicated a connection between trauma and our physical selves.

Benefits Body Awareness Offer

Being mindful of your body during treatment can help you better comprehend your body's signals and how they relate to your inner self. Changes in how you react to intense emotions can be facilitated by becoming aware of your breathing and other bodily sensations. For instance, you might not notice the bodily changes after a disagreement with a friend or coworker. Breathing more quickly, a beating heart, trembling, rigid limbs, stiffness, or a clenched jaw are examples of changes. After the conflict, you might see them, but you might not have noticed them then.

Imagine becoming more conscious of how your body reacts to unpleasant memories, unfavourable associations with objects around you, or conflicts with loved ones. A qualified somatic therapist can assist you in starting to become more aware of your body. They can support you throughout the session by encouraging you to pay attention to your body and any physical feelings. Learning about bodily sensations in a safe and supportive environment may help you develop, accept, and transform. Positivity affects your body and mind; you might be more balanced and liberated from its grip.

Since we are frequently the worst judges of ourselves, it is simpler to concentrate more on the behaviour, emotion, or response if we can objectively examine our bodies, that is, when our bodies don't do anything "good" or "bad." You can expect better results from your therapist when this element is included in the treatment. If you initially find this difficult, you can concentrate on other things. How frequently have you focused on a project with a deadline that you continued to work on despite your hunger? Similar to how it signals when it is agitated or nervous, your body lets you know when it needs sustenance. Being more conscious of your body's stress or overload indicators comes from paying more attention to your basic bodily demands. This enables you to make the connection between triggers you might miss when reacting to a painful experience or unsettling circumstance.

Working with a qualified somatic therapist will help you get an understanding of your body in addition to your mind and feelings.

Somatic therapists monitor mood and body language changes to identify indicators that may provide insight into underlying processes. To help you develop body awareness, we provide a vast array of body-based materials. Most of the human communication is nonverbal. Yes, we communicate with words, but our bodies speak volumes more. You are conversing even when sitting in a room with several people and remain silent. You could fidget without even realizing it if you're worried. You might not even know your jaw is locked if you are having a rough day. You can cross your arms across your chest more tightly.

Understanding the relationship between your emotions and your body fosters a strong mind-body connection, which clears the way for processing, acceptance, and self-awareness and improves your ability to react to your surroundings. You will have more good outcomes in therapy if you incorporate self-awareness into your sessions. It is a terrific ability to have and apply. Discuss other ideas or other strategies with your therapist if you are having trouble establishing a connection between your body and mind during treatment.

CHAPTER THREE

TECHNIQUES AND MODALITIES IN SOMATIC THERAPY

These methods differ and have some important commonalities. When it comes to using embodied awareness as a tool for healing, these five somatic therapies place a high value on a client's ability to recognize, name, and respond to bodily sensations that arise during a session. Their intended region of concentration is one of the models' primary differences. To treat attachment trauma—that is, the psychological impressions that early connections with carers or attachment figures leave on a person's sense of themselves and others—AEDP and Sensorimotor Psychotherapy were developed. In general, SE and EMDR emphasize nervous system control and the effects of certain traumatic situations, such as car accidents. Gestalt therapy primarily addresses relational and existential issues, such as how individuals may give their life meaning and purpose, rather than trauma-specific issues. A synopsis of each of these five somatic techniques is provided below. A particular emphasis is placed on how each method deals with physical trauma, the degree to which each approach is more organized or more impromptu, and the significance of the therapeutic alliance.

Overview of Various Somatic Therapy Approaches

Through bodily re-negotiation of previous experiences, the somatic method aims to release the body from intrusive pictures, thoughts, tension, panic, toxic relationships, and depressing or hopeless sentiments. Somatic work recognizes that prior experiences may become stuck in the body and works to release these manifestations by treating them somatically. Stated differently, the term somatic refers to relating to the body, and somatic treatment focuses on the mind-body relationship. Cognitive treatment methods, such as cognitive behavioural therapy (CBT), address difficulties verbally by focusing on your mental state. Psychologists practising somatic therapy view the body as a crucial component of our psychological well-being.

Some of the somatic therapy approaches include:

1. **Somatic Experiencing (SE)**

Focuses on addressing the effects of traumatic events. It was created by Peter Levine, who noticed that even while predators often menace wild animals, they usually recover their composure following such assaults by quivering and shrugging off their "charged" adrenaline. Levine observed that following a traumatic event, a lot of people find it more difficult to let go of this charged energy and instead store the post-traumatic stress in their body, which manifests as tense muscles, a racing heart, or numbness. To help clients release this stored physical energy, SE assists them in learning about their autonomic nervous system. The goal of SE therapy is to help clients learn how to "pendulate," or switch between the different nervous system states of feeling charged and calm, so they can learn how to soothe themselves more skillfully. This means that SE frequently does not require clients to process a particular trauma fully.

Through various activities, SE practitioners assist clients in tracking their bodily feelings. Numerous SE practitioners have also received training in touch work, so if clients are willing, they may utilize touch to communicate more directly with their nervous systems.

Clients using Somatic Experiencing receive help learning about their autonomic nervous system to free this congealed bodily energy.

2. **Experiential Dynamic Psychotherapy (AEDP)**

Hold that our basic emotions—grief, anger, fear, joy, disgust, and excitement—are essentially good and, when completely processed, may naturally lead us toward transformation, development, and healing.

However, when we encounter "unbearable loneliness due to overwhelming emotions," many of us suffer in our interpersonal interactions. By "undoing" the client's aloneness during sessions, AEDP therapists assist clients in processing these fundamental emotional sensations in a fresh, secure, and healthy way, therefore healing such attachment traumas. AEDP therapists have a distinct viewpoint in which they see their therapeutic alliance as the main means of promoting healing. As deeply uplifting as they are, AEDP therapists bring their felt experiences into sessions rather than instructing clients to control their feelings from the sidelines. As with Sensorimotor Psychotherapy or Gestalt, AEDP therapists can assist clients in exploring basic emotional experiences by responding to the bodily sensations that arise naturally throughout the therapy. AEDP therapists see their therapeutic alliance as the main means of promoting recovery.

3. **Sensorimotor Psychotherapy**

Our bodies are tracked for patterns and habits derived from early attachment bonds and prior experiences. According to studies on mirror neurons, learning happens in the body before it is incorporated into our mind. The goal of Sensorimotor Psychotherapy, as established by Pat Ogden, who was significantly affected by The Hakomi Method, is to particularly treat the effects of attachment trauma and how it is stored in an individual's body, postures, and emotional experiences. Sensorimotor psychotherapy aims to help clients understand how embracing a positive attitude alters their felt experience by addressing how limiting cognitive beliefs—like feeling unlovable—are handled in the body. The goal of interventions is to help the client understand the relationship between their impulses, gestures, and movements and their attachment requirements.

4. **Eye Movement Desensitization and Reprocessing (EMDR)**

Focuses on traumatic experiences and how they are stored in the central nervous system. In contrast to many other trauma therapies, EMDR uses "bilateral stimulation" to address a painful memory directly and alter its neural representation. When you focus on a particular memory, bilateral stimulation refers to moving your entire body in a pattern of motion that stimulates both sides of the brain.

Examples include alternately tapping your left and right leg or shifting your gaze from left to right. Compared to the other therapies on this list, EMDR is a more regulated method with standardized output. In contrast with several other trauma treatment options, EMDR uses "bilateral stimulation" to address a painful memory directly and alter its neural representation.

5. **Gestalt Therapy**

This comprehensive method emphasizes the present moment and helps individuals release protective tendencies that impede their innate capacity to access their energy. Gestalt accepts the "paradoxical theory of change," which holds that individuals change when they have a profound awareness of who they are rather than when they try to change. The 1950s saw the establishment of Gestalt, a process-oriented method that impacted the growth of modalities like AEDP and Sensorimotor Psychotherapy. In contrast, Gestalt focuses on helping clients find meaning and purpose in their lives rather than on attachment trauma as a specialized speciality. To uncover the underlying emotions of their clients, Gestalt practitioners, such as those who practice AEDP and Sensorimotor Psychotherapy, keep an eye on their clients' body language, gestures, and noises while concentrating on the present.

Similarly to AEDP, Gestalt practitioners facilitate deeper emotional processing for their clients using impromptu "experiments" such as asking them to amplify a phrase or action. Gestalt therapists sometimes encourage clients to exaggerate a movement or a statement to facilitate deeper emotional processing. Although there are several somatic treatments, they all use the body and bodily feelings in the therapeutic process.

Any of these five alternative ways may be the most appropriate for you, depending on what you're seeking healing from a specific traumatic event, childhood traumas, or existential problems.

Embodiment Practices (Breathwork, Movement, Touch)

In embodiment practices, self-awareness, mindfulness, connection, self-regulation, achieving balance, and developing self-acceptance are tools for healing via the body. The link between our energy and physical selves is examined through embodiment. It entails how our bodies, minds, and behaviours interact. Progressive muscular relaxation, dance or movement therapy, visualization, and sensory awareness are often used in embodiment practices. To accelerate the healing process, a client may be asked to notice sensations while discussing themes in psychotherapy sessions that include embodiment practices. Practices of embodiment are included in the field of somatic psychology. The premise of somatic psychology is:

- Experiences affect our physical, emotional, mental, and spiritual well-being.

- Our sensory systems must process every occurrence.

- Not only do thoughts originate in the mind, but they also happen physiologically throughout the body.

The development of embodiment involves the fusion of the following sensory feedback systems:

- Exteroception is the process by which the brain receives information about the outside world through the body's sense organs (eyes, ears, nose, tongue, and skin). A mindfulness practice that emphasizes focusing on certain sensations might be an excellent illustration of this.

- The term "proprioception" describes the body's sensory response to gravitation. The brain receives sensory data from the body's joints and inner ear through neurons, which results in proprioception. Examples of this might be yoga poses or dance-based embodiment exercises.

- The interior body's sensory experiences are a part of interoception. It might involve sensations of tension, discomfort, hunger, thirst, and body temperature. Sensory nerve cells, which transmit data from muscles, organs, and tissue connections to the brain, enhance the provision of feedback on emotional events. An excellent illustration of this would be mindful eating practice.

Theory and Philosophy of Embodiment

The philosophy and theory of embodiment suggest that the body's sensory systems and cognitive processes are intertwined, with the mind playing a central role. According to these views, thinking about a thing or someone causes the experience to be simulated. Embodiment philosophy is supported by neuroscience; research shows that the mere act of thinking about faces, music, flavours, odours, and other items causes the brain to activate in a way that corresponds to the body. The body acts as a medium via which the brain directs contact with the outside environment. The embodiment theory's fundamental principle is that the body affects every psychological activity, including emotions, motor functions, and sensory perception. Education psychology, social psychology, neuroscience, clinical psychology, and cognitive and social development theories concur with this.

Putting theory and philosophy aside, the following three embodiment practices are instances:

- **Managing Depression:** Treatment for depression can benefit greatly from the use of embodied approaches. Studies have indicated that talk therapy alone is not as helpful as mindfulness-based cognitive therapy in treating depression and avoiding recurrence. Clients may monitor and gain control over their feedback by including grounding methods, awareness of bodily sensations, and physiological reactions to certain ideas. Additionally, via energetic exercise, hard activities, and happy music, clients may discover physiological strategies to improve activation, energy, and good thinking.

- **Handling Anxiety:** Through the process of clearing their brains, embodiment practices are an excellent means of treating anxiety in patients. Most discussions of anxiety refer to the "fight or flight" reaction, which is the body's physiological and biochemical reaction to environmental stimuli brought on by an inaccurate perception of the brain. In a state known as "hypofrontality," the prefrontal cortex—responsible for reasoning and analysis—goes offline due to an overload of sensory data. This is what happens during anxiety.

Through physical challenge and engagement and a reduction in excessive mental activity, embodiment practices can help lessen anxious thoughts and foster a stronger sense of empowerment and tranquillity. Another way to biologically reprogram the parasympathetic nervous system not to activate the fight-or-flight response is through physical activity.

- **Using Embodiment to Treat Eating Disorders:** People who suffer from eating disorders have lost touch with who they are and how they look. They no longer attend to, listen to, or react to their bodies' cues. Intense emotions might be momentarily distracted from and briefly relieved by eating problem behaviours. Individuals with an eating disorder are taught via embodiment practices to accept themselves as they are and to establish a relationship with their body and mind that allows for recovery.

Among the embodiment techniques investigated the most for treating eating problems is yoga. A month following therapy, the symptoms of the individualized yoga group showed more recovery than those of the control group, which was getting standard treatment for eating disorders. Researchers found that yoga therapy is a useful addition to conventional treatment for eating disorders since food obsession also considerably decreased following all yoga sessions.

Five Restorative Activities for Your Sessions

An embodiment exercise can be any movement or attention to bodily feeling. It's important to complete the task attentively and pay attention to your senses (smell, sight, touch, taste, and sound). Engaging the senses, going slowly, and allowing oneself to connect more deeply to one's body and the experience may help clients use common activities like baking, cooking, and gardening as therapeutic aids. Here are some suggestions on how to include embodiment in counselling or psychotherapy sessions:

- Start the session with a mindful breathing practice to assist the client centre and establish a connection between the mind and body.

- Discuss how the sensations relate to whatever the client is going through as you take the group for a mindful walk in the grass while wearing no shoes.

- Stretching for the upper body and neck is simple to perform in an office, so include a little stretching period.

Moving Treatment Via Dance

The foundation of dance therapy is the notion that the body and mind are interconnected and that dancing may have a healing effect when combined with psychotherapy techniques. Dance can enhance emotional, social, cognitive, and physical integration to enhance health and wellness. Dancing offers more aspects of embodiment-based therapy because of its intricate movement, rhythm, and sensory features. Hedonism (non-goal-oriented pleasure), aesthetic experience, expressive communication, creativity, and particular bodily feedback processes about movement, form, and physical feeling are all included in this therapeutic approach.

Illustration: According to a neuroscience study, visualizing an experience—whether aural or physical—activates the same brain regions as experiencing it. Images, noises, pressure, and body motions may all trigger the senses of sight, hearing, touch, and space. Our perception of the world around us is a combination of our senses rather than a single, objective process. Therefore, when physical movement is not an option, visualization may be a very effective healing technique. Clients, for instance, might see themselves sitting in an office and taking a stroll outdoors. Even those who can't dance to music might imagine the noises, movements, and sensations they could encounter if they could.

Increasing Ease of Muscular Relaxing

Tensing and relaxing a set of muscles with breathing (inhale as you tense, exhale as you release) is known as progressive muscle relaxation. A lot of data supports the claims that this method enhances body awareness, reduces tension, and promotes physical relaxation. Clients can learn to identify the locations of their stored muscular tension and how to physically release it by methodically working on every part of the body. Anxiety is far less likely to occur when the body is physiologically at ease. You may find mental health books and audio instructions that can lead you through a gradual muscle relaxation exercise.

Yoga & Embodiment

Yoga includes the physical practice of "asanas," or poses, and pranayama. As was previously noted, poses and movements are intended to support healing and health by easing physical, mental, and psychological pain. Yoga poses and movement styles encourage people to become aware of their experiences without passing judgment. An intense link between the mind, body, and soul is formed by the increased awareness of the posture and its sensation. Yoga is a highly researched embodiment therapy that provides an ideal mind-body practice for fostering connection. Yoga may help clients let go of preconceived notions about what a pose "should" be and compare themselves to others by focusing on the sensation of the postures and movement rather than their appearance. It can be achieved through breathing, postures, and moment-to-moment mindfulness. Certain yoga poses are said to provide relief for emotions, conditions, and problems. For instance, it is believed that inversions—head below hips—help direct energy into the heart, enhance vitality, and encourage emotional recovery.

How to Apply Breathwork

Breathwork, or "pranayama," is an essential component of the embodiment practice in yoga. Breathwork isn't very sophisticated in its manifestation, though. You must practice different breathing techniques while keeping your awareness and concentration on your breath. Breath work focuses on an essential aspect of human life and establishes an instantaneous link between the mind and body.

Breathwork examples include:

- Breathing in three parts: filling the chest, ribs, and abdomen, then exhaling similarly.

- Breathe in square motion for four counts, hold it for four counts, exhale it for four counts, hold it for four counts, etc.

- Breathe diaphragmatically while lying down and using your breath to make a light item, like a book, rise and fall on your diaphragm.

Body-mind Integration Exercises

People may develop awareness, trust their bodies as trustworthy information sources and learn safe emotional expression techniques by practising body-mind integration. And to anticipate a happier existence because of an integrated brain, sympathetic connections, and cohesive thinking. For all of this, a well-articulated body-based strategy is necessary. Integration in the context of the brain refers to the process by which distinct regions of the skull and the body, each with its functions, connect via synaptic connections. More complex procedures, including insight, empathy, intuition, coordination, emotional equilibrium, grace, and morality, might arise because of these integrated links. Integration in an individual's mind is the connection of disparate mental processes, such as reasoning with emotion and feeling with the body.

The first step in healing a person's body is to release the tensions that, like vaulted arches, connect various psychosomatic symptoms and closed wounds. Then, integration—which entails connecting all the body's previously mostly unconscious major dimensions—

begins with the coordination and unification of the entire self within the body. More room is made available for "the alive" and the roll call of the living because of their release and assimilation into the soma. Body-mind Integration assists individuals in rediscovering and evolving into their true selves. Combining client-centred attitudes and concepts from system-oriented, cognitive-behavioural, and psychodynamic psychology into a single integrated philosophy is known as body-mind integration. The most recent data on the evolutionary history of human psychology and physiology provide credence to this cohesive approach.

Utilizing well-defined concepts and methodologies, body/mind knowledge and experiences are delivered to clients in a way that allows them to maintain control over their therapy process. It helps the clients meet their long-standing needs for filling psychological development gaps. Essentially, the practitioner of body-mind integration sessions creates a place devoid of judgment or attempts at "cure," respectfully permitting the exploration and fuller experience of "what is." The client's innate intelligence is developed and enhanced in this way. The "essential self," or intrinsic health, is the centre of attention.

Emotions, sensations, thoughts, and memories are all part of the body-mind connections. To progressively get a deeper understanding of the mind-body connections inside themselves, clients "dive" into themselves. This enhances the interaction between experienced sensations, pictures, ideas, spoken words, and shared and expressed emotions. Alongside preexisting imprints, the client absorbs new sensory-motor, kinesthetic, and auditory-visual memories. The availability of substitute synthetic memories will foster more positive expectations and behaviour and more realistic viewpoints on oneself and other people, increasing happiness, fulfilment, significance, and closeness in the present.

Case Studies Illustrating Techniques

Here we will share two (2) examples of rape victims as described by their therapist:

Case Study 1: Johanns

Johanna B., the client, began her Body Psychotherapy procedure at the age of forty. She and her two kids had lived alone after their divorce two years earlier. She had taken psychology courses but never received her degree. Her professional career came to an abrupt halt when her treating physician declared that she had "advanced fibromyalgia." Feeling down due to her illness and still going through a divorce, she went to a psychotherapist for assistance.

Spouse. Her mistrust had also caused the attempt to start a new relationship with a different man to fail. Thus, it took us a long time to establish a safe space for each other when we first started treatment. It seemed like she had to put our connection to the test anytime she sensed sentiments of trust before she could say it was "safe." It was beneficial for her to feel this distrust in our relationship since she observed it without repercussions. In her personal life, an additional endeavour to establish a romantic connection with a guy significantly deteriorated her emotional state.

The woman mentioned experiencing panic episodes and persistent discomfort as traumatic effects. She believed that she was abandoned and defenceless by her spouse. Her mistrust had also caused the attempt to start a new relationship with a different man to fail. Thus, it took us a long time to establish a safe space for each other when we first started treatment. It seemed like she had to put our connection to the test anytime she sensed sentiments of trust before she could say it was "safe."

It was beneficial for her to sense this distrust in our relationship since she observed it without repercussions. In her personal life, an additional endeavour to establish a romantic connection with a guy significantly deteriorated her emotional state. Johanns said that her body was hurting much more. We started by "mindfully" examining her symptoms and managing some. In addition to her physical ailments, she had, for the first time, connected with vague childhood recollections of sexual and violent assault. She was starting to relive the terrible things that had happened to her father when she was little.

Her spouse later experienced the same things. She had been the Victim of both mental and physical abuse in both instances. Her position is shown via a dream: As per my old habits, I woke up sweating in the middle of the night. My hair stuck, too. Wet all over my neck. I was in excruciating pain. It seemed like I had died, as though the anguish in my arms and legs had frozen. I was hurt by everything. My spouse informed me that he had taken his rightful share. I sensed how my dread prevented me from speaking or expressing myself.

It was challenging for me to try to deal with her physical symptoms more. She kept going into the realm of her thoughts rather than engaging in her physical realities. I saw my customer becoming slightly irritated with this apparent lack of cooperation. However, my client was also angry that I was placing any pressure on her. As we discussed our problems, she confided in me about the violent incidents and sexual abuse she had experienced as a youngster. Not only could I sense her anxiousness and worry, but I could also sense her fury. I assisted her in piecing together some of her suppressed recollections during our subsequent encounters. We now knew far more about her motivations.

We gained a better understanding of her fears and the significance of her naming every memory piece. My role was to assist her in managing her nearly excessive energy as she reassembled her memories. A little clip might serve as an example of this work's component: Therapist (TH) and client (CL):

(TH) Observing your father approaching you while you access your inner kid, what senses do you have in your body?

• (CL) I'm a little afraid.

• (TH) What part of your body is experiencing this type of fear?

• (CL) My gut feels constricted right there.

• (TH) It's alright. Just remain with this constricted sensation for a little while.

When you stick with it, what happens next.?

As I explained this, I noticed that my entire body began shaking. I then advised her to learn to remain with the shaking sensations by concentrating on them. She discovered from the previous sessions that she could tolerate these uncomfortable sensations until they subsided, at which point her body would feel more at ease. We generally adhered to this order to create a methodology that lets us operate with episodic memory. Using this procedure, I enquired: Select one instance when there are no signs of trauma, only stress.

Containment entails maintaining attention on the feeling until the body regulates it. Recall the incident and ask them to describe it in more detail until they exhibit symptoms. At this point, you should help them put it behind them so they can regain self-control and begin to monitor their body's movements and feelings.

Close by discussing "Resourcing" and what the customer can do next. The therapist and the client can develop confidence in their internal bodily responses by adhering to this kind of regimen. In addition, they can recognize that, following a trauma, people often behave differently in relationships, making the therapy relationship a valuable setting for experimenting with various relationship techniques. Consequently, they may find it harder to trust people "Will you harm me?" or to protect themselves ("Please don't harm me!").

A trauma therapist's primary responsibility is generally to assist clients in regaining their capacity for trust, particularly regarding setting and defending boundaries. Trauma therapists are also trained to deal with circumstances of traumatic transference, such as "You just sit there and watch me suffer", "You'll save me", or "You can understand me because this happened to you, too." "I don't trust you," or "You don't care about me."

Discussion

While most of the trauma literature focuses on the "Victims'" post-traumatic symptoms, each post-traumatic role has its own set of symptoms. Compassion weariness can be shown by "rescuers." Both "rescuers" and "bystanders" may experience stress related to "observing" or survivor guilt. The "Perpetrators" experience the most extreme post-traumatic dysfunctions, such as addiction, suicide, and maybe re-enactment. All persons present, however, may experience some degree of post-traumatic symptoms if they are exposed to any current traumatic incident. People "remember" what they perceive to have been the experiences of the other people there at the horrific incident, which makes trauma transference conceivable. Like how we picture others' experiences in daily empathetic interactions, we do this to build rapport, comprehend people, and get insight into how they may behave. In the process of healing from trauma, we also absorb what we believe to have been the experiences of others who were not directly involved in the incident.

Whatever actions we may have engaged in ourselves, as therapists, we must educate ourselves on all possible behaviours: those of the Victim, Perpetrator, Rescuer, and Bystander. Through this process, we understand these four distinct "orientations" towards the world: how the world seems different when we are a Bystander, a Victim, a Rescuer, or a Perpetrator. All these post-traumatic "stances" or postures are taught to us. Recognizing and incorporating all four post-traumatic roles is necessary for healing.

How does this apply to therapy? To alleviate these symptoms, we must integrate the memory of each of the four possible "roles" (Victim, perpetrator, rescuer, and bystander) as though we were each of them. Idealistically, the bystander should be able to integrate the experience of the Victim, the perpetrator should be able to incorporate the experience of the rescuer, and the Victim should be able to integrate the (previously imagined) experience of the perpetrator.

Case study 2

A seven-year-old child who had been sexually molested only knew that his body was numb. His body seemed immobile. He went into a state of awareness by closing his eyes and following his therapist's instructions. He spoke quite emotively about his dread and his desire for protection as he began to see his cousin entering the room. His legs grew tense and started to tremble. With empathy, his therapist joined him and put her hands on his legs, holding them in place to keep him secure. He relaxed and began to shiver because of her protection by applying pressure to his legs and being a soothing presence in the mutually beneficial bond.

The therapist leading the conceptualization said that the nervous system was biologically digesting information that it could not process during the danger. After shaking for a few minutes, the boy's emotional and biological reaction ended when he slowed down and stopped. In the subsequent session, he reported feeling less rigid and heavier, and he could sense the feelings in his body with a greater awareness of them.

CHAPTER FOUR

APPLICATIONS & BENEFITS

Somatic Therapy in Clinical Practice

Somatic therapy, a dynamic and evolving field in mental health, has gained significant recognition for its unique approach to healing by incorporating the wisdom of the body into therapeutic practices. In clinical settings, where the mind-body connection is pivotal to comprehensive well-being, somatic therapy emerges as a transformative force. This article delves into the nuanced aspects of somatic therapy in clinical practice, exploring its principles, techniques, and the profound impact it can have on individuals seeking holistic healing.

At the core of somatic therapy lies the belief that the body and mind are intricately interconnected. Understanding the body's language becomes crucial in unravelling the complexities of emotional and psychological distress. Somatic therapists recognize that the body often retains and expresses the imprints of past traumas and experiences, manifesting in physical sensations, tension, or discomfort. Therapists aim to facilitate a holistic healing process by acknowledging and addressing these bodily responses.

The Therapeutic Alliance:

Establishing a strong therapeutic alliance between the client and therapist is paramount in the clinical application of somatic therapy. Unlike traditional talk therapies, somatic therapy invites individuals to explore bodily sensations, emotions, and memories. This requires a high degree of trust and rapport as clients are guided through an intimate journey of self-discovery. By training in somatic techniques, therapists create a safe and supportive environment that encourages open communication and vulnerability.

Embodied Awareness and Mindfulness:

Central to somatic therapy is the cultivation of embodied awareness – the practice of being fully present in the moment and attuned to one's bodily sensations. This mindfulness aspect is a powerful tool in clinical settings, allowing individuals to connect with their internal experiences. Therapists guide clients in developing the capacity to observe and tolerate bodily sensations without judgment, fostering a sense of self-acceptance and resilience in the face of emotional challenges.

Body-Centered Techniques:

Somatic therapy encompasses an array of body-centred techniques designed to engage and release physical tension, trauma, and emotional blockages. These may include breathwork, movement exercises, and touch-based interventions. For instance, breathwork techniques such as deep diaphragmatic breathing can help regulate the nervous system, promoting relaxation conducive to therapeutic exploration. Movement-based practices, such as dance or yoga, offer avenues for expressing and releasing stored emotions nonverbally.

Integration into Daily Life:

Somatic therapy extends beyond the confines of therapy sessions, encouraging individuals to integrate its principles into their daily lives. Therapists collaborate with clients to develop personalized self-care practices and exercises that promote ongoing embodied awareness. This integration empowers individuals to actively participate in their healing journey actively, fostering a sense of agency and resilience outside the therapeutic space.

Neurobiological Considerations:

Somatic therapy aligns with advancements in neurobiology, acknowledging the plasticity of the brain and its capacity for change. Neuroscientific research supports the idea that therapeutic interventions focused on the body can reshape neural pathways, promoting emotional resilience and well-being. Somatic therapists leverage this understanding to tailor interventions that address immediate symptoms and contribute to long-term neurobiological changes.

Cultural Adaptation

In the diverse landscape of clinical practice, somatic therapy recognizes and respects cultural nuances. Therapists consider how cultural backgrounds influence individuals' relationships with their bodies and emotions. Culturally sensitive somatic interventions are designed to honour and integrate diverse perspectives, fostering a therapeutic space that is inclusive and attuned to each client's unique experiences.

Future Trends:

As somatic therapy evolves, future trends emphasize increased collaboration between somatic and traditional therapeutic modalities. Integrating somatic principles into mainstream mental health practices holds the potential to usher in a new era of holistic and client-centred care. In conclusion, the marriage of somatic therapy with clinical practice represents a groundbreaking approach, bridging the gap between body and mind to unlock the full spectrum of human healing potential.

Addressing Trauma and PTSD:

Trauma, whether acute or chronic, can significantly impact emotional regulation and resilience. Somatic therapy provides a gentle and effective avenue for addressing trauma by working with the body's inherent wisdom. Therapeutic modalities like Somatic Experiencing (SE) and Trauma Release Exercises (TRE) specifically target trauma stored in the body, allowing individuals to release and regulate overwhelming emotions.

Through a gradual and mindful process, somatic therapy empowers individuals to renegotiate their relationship with trauma. By fostering a sense of safety within the body and promoting self-regulation, individuals can embark on a transformative journey toward increased emotional resilience.

One of the most notable applications of somatic therapy in clinical practice is its effectiveness in addressing trauma and post-traumatic stress disorder (PTSD). Traumatic experiences often become lodged in the body's cellular memory, leading to chronic tension and emotional dysregulation. Somatic therapists employ gentle and gradual interventions to help individuals renegotiate their relationship with these stored traumas. By engaging the body's natural self-regulating mechanisms, somatic therapy supports clients in reclaiming a sense of safety and empowerment.

Trauma, in its various forms, can leave indelible imprints on the human psyche, affecting the mind and deeply embedding itself within the body. Post-Traumatic Stress Disorder (PTSD), a consequence of severe trauma, manifests not only as vivid memories and emotional distress but also as a somatic experience. In recent years, the field of mental health has seen a growing recognition of the importance of addressing trauma through a holistic lens, leading to the emergence of somatic therapy as a powerful modality for healing. This article delves into the intricate connection between trauma, PTSD, and the innovative ways somatic therapy engages the body to facilitate profound healing and recovery.

Understanding the Trauma-Body Connection

At the core of somatic therapy's effectiveness in treating trauma lies the understanding that trauma is not just a mental phenomenon but an embodied experience. Traumatic events often result in a dysregulation of the nervous system, leaving a person in a constant state of hyperarousal or hypo-arousal. This dysregulation, in turn, affects the body's ability to process and release the intense energy associated with trauma. Somatic therapy recognizes the intricate dance between the mind and body, acknowledging that trauma resides not only in memories and thoughts but also in the very cells and tissues of the body.

The Neurobiology of Trauma and Somatic Experiences

To comprehend how somatic therapy addresses trauma and PTSD, it is crucial to explore the neurobiological underpinnings of these experiences. Trauma often results in alterations in the brain's structure and function, particularly in areas associated with threat detection and emotional processing. Somatic therapy engages with these neurological changes by incorporating practices regulating the autonomic nervous system, promoting safety and relaxation. Techniques such as breathwork, mindfulness, and body awareness exercises become vehicles for rewiring the neural pathways affected by trauma, fostering resilience, and facilitating recovery.

Embodiment Practices in Somatic Therapy

Incorporating embodiment practices is Central to somatic therapy's efficacy in addressing trauma. These practices involve reconnecting individuals with their bodies fostering an awareness of sensations, movements, and the present moment. Breathwork, for instance, becomes a powerful tool for grounding and centring, helping individuals navigate the overwhelming emotions associated with trauma. Movement-based practices, such as yoga or dance therapy, provide avenues for expressing and releasing pent-up energy stored in the body. The intentional focus on the body allows individuals to reclaim a sense of agency and safety, critical elements in the healing journey from trauma.

Case Studies: Illuminating the Impact of Somatic Techniques

Real-world examples often provide a tangible understanding of the transformative power of somatic therapy. Consider the case of Sarah, a survivor of a violent assault who struggled with debilitating flashbacks and hypervigilance. Traditional talk therapy alone proved insufficient in addressing the visceral nature of her trauma. Through somatic therapy, Sarah learned to identify and regulate the sensations in her body associated with triggers. Grounding techniques, such as feeling the support of the chair or the sensation of her feet on the ground, became anchors during moments of distress. Over time, Sarah experienced a profound shift in her relationship with her body and her ability to navigate the world without being constantly haunted by the past.

Enhancing Emotional Regulation and Resilience

Emotional regulation is recognizing, understanding, and healthily managing our emotions. It's like having a remote control for our feelings – being able to turn down the volume when things get too overwhelming. To enhance emotional regulation, start by identifying your emotions. Ask yourself, "What am I feeling right now?" This simple question can be a powerful first step towards better emotional awareness.

Breathing Techniques

Mindful breathing is one of the easiest and most effective ways to regulate emotions. When we're stressed or upset, our breathing tends to become shallow. Take a moment to inhale deeply through your nose, hold for a few seconds, and then exhale slowly through your mouth. This calms the nervous system and provides a moment of clarity to assess the situation with a more level-headed approach.

Positive Self-Talk

Our internal dialogue significantly influences our emotions. Pay attention to the way you speak to yourself. Instead of dwelling on negative thoughts, practice positive self-talk. For example, if you make a mistake, rather than saying, "I'm so stupid," try saying, "I made a mistake, but I can learn from it." This shift in mindset can foster resilience and help you bounce back from challenges.

Establishing Healthy Habits

Physical health and emotional well-being are closely connected. Engage in regular physical activity, eat nutritious meals, and ensure you get enough sleep. These habits contribute to a stable emotional foundation, making it easier to handle stress and adversity. A healthy body often translates to a healthy mind.

Building a Support System

Resilience is not about facing challenges alone; it's about having a support network. Share your feelings with friends, family, or a trusted confidant. Talking about emotions can be therapeutic and provide different perspectives on situations. Additionally, seeking professional help, such as counselling, can be a valuable resource for developing emotional resilience.

Mindfulness and Meditation

Practising mindfulness and meditation can significantly enhance emotional regulation. Set aside a few minutes each day to focus on the present moment. This can be as simple as paying attention to your breath, the sensations in your body, or the sounds around you. These practices promote self-awareness, allowing you to respond to emotions consciously rather than reactively.

Emotional regulation and resilience are essential tools for navigating the ups and downs in life. By incorporating simple yet powerful techniques such as mindful breathing, positive self-talk, healthy habits, building a support system, and practising mindfulness, you can empower yourself to face challenges with greater emotional balance. Remember, it's okay to seek help when needed, and each step towards enhancing emotional well-being is a step towards a more fulfilling and resilient life.

Cultural Considerations and Diversity in Somatic Therapy

Cultural diversity encompasses many factors, including ethnicity, race, gender, sexual orientation, socioeconomic status, etc. In the context of somatic theory, practitioners must be attuned to the diverse backgrounds of their clients to create a safe and inclusive space for healing. Different cultures may have distinct approaches to expressing and experiencing emotions, pain, and trauma. Sensitivity to these cultural nuances ensures that somatic interventions resonate with individuals from various backgrounds.

Language and Communication

Language is a powerful tool that reflects cultural norms and values. Practitioners must be mindful of linguistic nuances, as certain words or expressions may carry different meanings across cultures. Clear and open communication is fundamental in somatic therapy, and practitioners should be adaptable in their choice of language to ensure that clients feel understood and respected.

Cultural Competence in Practice

Cultural competence involves understanding, appreciating, and effectively working with individuals from diverse cultural backgrounds. Somatic practitioners must undergo ongoing training to enhance their cultural competence, enabling them to navigate the complexities of diverse client experiences. This may include staying informed about cultural practices, traditions, and belief systems that influence individuals' somatic experiences.

Tailoring Interventions

The somatic theory emphasizes personalized interventions based on individual experiences and needs. Cultural and diversity considerations demand that practitioners tailor their approaches to accommodate the unique backgrounds of their clients. This might involve integrating cultural practices, rituals, or mindfulness techniques that resonate with the client's heritage, fostering a deeper connection between the individual and the therapeutic process.

Addressing Trauma Through a Cultural Lens

Trauma is a universal human experience, yet its manifestations and impacts vary across cultures. Somatic practitioners must recognize the cultural dimensions of trauma, acknowledging that certain events may carry different weight and significance for individuals from diverse backgrounds. By adopting a culturally informed approach to trauma, practitioners can provide more nuanced and effective support for their clients.

In the evolving landscape of somatic theory, cultural and diversity considerations are integral to the success of therapeutic interventions. A culturally sensitive approach respects individual differences and enhances the effectiveness of somatic practices by acknowledging the intricate interplay between culture, identity, and healing. Somatic practitioners must commit to ongoing education, adaptability, and a genuine appreciation for the richness of human diversity to create inclusive spaces that promote holistic well-being for all. As we navigate the intricate tapestry of human experiences, weaving cultural awareness into the fabric of somatic theory is a crucial step toward fostering a more equitable and compassionate approach to healing.

CHAPTER FIVE

INTEGRATION AND PERSONAL GROWTH

Integrating Somatic Techniques into Daily Life

Including somatic techniques in your daily routine doesn't have to be difficult or time-consuming. These straightforward yet effective methods can improve your health by helping you establish a stronger bond between your body and mind. You're taking care of yourself and your feeling of presence when you embrace moments of mindfulness, breath awareness, and gentle movement. Remember that the flexibility of somatic activities allows you to customize them to your schedule and tastes. You'll discover that you can handle life's obstacles more efficiently and develop a long-lasting inner calm as you progressively apply these techniques.

Comprehending Somatic Activities:

Somatic practices emphasize the value of paying attention to body cues and experiences centred around the wisdom of the body-mind link. These methods include mindfulness, body scan meditation, moderate movement, and breathwork. The goals include promoting self-awareness, releasing tension, and achieving a harmonious balance between your emotional and physical states.

The Body's Wisdom:

At the heart of somatic therapy lies the recognition that our bodies carry a wealth of wisdom. Every experience, emotion, and trauma is encoded in our physical being. Yet, in the hustle and bustle of our lives, we often find ourselves detached from these bodily sensations. "Integrating Somatic Techniques into Daily Life" explores reclaiming this lost connection and leveraging the body's inherent wisdom for a more balanced and fulfilling existence.

Mindful Embodiment in Action:

Imagine a day where your movements, breath, and sensations are not just mundane routines but gateways to self-discovery and healing. This is the essence of integrating somatic techniques into daily life. Through mindfulness practices, breathwork, and gentle movement exercises, individuals can learn to fully inhabit their bodies, fostering a heightened awareness of the present moment.

Transforming Stress into Resilience:

One of the primary benefits of incorporating somatic techniques into our daily routines is the ability to transform stress into resilience. By attuning to the body's subtle signals, individuals can intercept stress responses before they escalate, promoting a more adaptive and calm nervous system. This shift not only enhances emotional well-being but also contributes to improved physical health.

Beyond Therapy: Practical Applications:

While somatic therapy has its roots in therapeutic settings, the beauty lies in its accessibility for everyone. "Integrating Somatic Techniques into Daily Life" delves into practical applications for individuals from all walks of life. From simple mindfulness exercises to incorporating body awareness into mundane activities, this chapter explores how somatic techniques can be seamlessly woven into the fabric of our everyday experiences.

A Journey of Personal Growth:

Integrating somatic techniques isn't just a collection of exercises; it's a transformative journey toward personal growth. By consistently engaging with the body's signals, individuals can unravel patterns, release stored tension, and cultivate a deeper understanding of themselves. This chapter explores how these practices contribute to an ongoing process of self-discovery and personal evolution.

Self-Care Practices and Exercises

It might be difficult to find times of peace and self-awareness in the busyness of modern life. Somatic activities are a powerful method to reestablish a connection with your body, lower stress levels, and improve general well-being. While attending therapy sessions is important, incorporating somatic activities into your everyday routine can increase the advantages and promote a more comprehensive healing process. The good news is that it's quite simple to include somatic techniques into your daily routine. Let's discuss how including somatic activities in your daily routine can help you feel more present, connected, and at peace with yourself.

- **Morning Intentional Breathing**

Take a few minutes to focus on your breathing to start your day. Locate a peaceful area, sit comfortably, and shut your eyes. Breathe deeply through your nose, causing your belly to swell. Breathe slowly through your mouth to release any tension or concerns. Continue letting each breath anchor you in the here and now.

- **Pauses for Mindful Movement**

Throughout the day, take brief, mindful movement breaks. Get up, stretch, and pay attention to your body's feelings. You can roll your shoulders, gently twist your torso, or perform a quick head-to-toe body scan. These bursts of activity can revitalize you and keep your body and mind from becoming stagnant.

- **Somatic Inspections**

Set aside a short time before bed or during your lunch break to perform a somatic check-in. As you lay there comfortably, mentally go over your entire body, from head to toe. Take note of any places that are tense, uncomfortable, or relaxed. Breathe into the tight spots and picture yourself letting go of any pent-up tension.

- **Conscious Eating**

Turn eating into a sensual experience. Breathe deeply a few times and use all your senses before eating. Take note of your food's flavours, textures, and colours. Chew gently and enjoy every taste, paying attention to how food feels on your tongue and body.

- **Relaxation Ritual Before Bed**

Before going to bed, practice somatic relaxation. Shut your eyes, lie in bed, and inhale deeply a few times. Your head should be the last muscle group to relax after gradually tensing and releasing each toe. As your body sinks into the mattress, welcome the sensation of peace that overtakes you.

Future Trends in Somatic Therapy

Somatic therapy, a dynamic field that explores the interconnectedness of the mind and body in the healing process, has witnessed significant growth and acceptance in recent years. As we stand at the cusp of a new era, it's essential to explore future trends that may shape the landscape of somatic therapy. These emerging trends reflect advancements in scientific understanding and respond to the evolving needs of individuals seeking holistic approaches to well-being.

Embodied Technology: Bridging the Virtual and the Physical

One prominent trend on the horizon is integrating technology into somatic therapy practices. With the rise of virtual reality (VR) and augmented reality (AR), therapists are exploring ways to incorporate these immersive experiences to enhance somatic healing. Virtual environments can simulate real-life situations, providing a safe space for individuals to confront and process trauma. Additionally, wearable devices and biofeedback tools may offer real-time data on physiological responses, allowing therapists to tailor interventions based on individual needs and progress.

Neuroscientific Advancements: Unraveling the Mysteries of the Brain-Body Connection

The future of somatic therapy is closely tied to ongoing developments in neuroscience. As our understanding of the brain-body connection deepens, somatic therapists may increasingly leverage neuroscientific insights to refine and customize treatment approaches. Techniques directly targeting neural pathways involved in emotional regulation and trauma processing could become more prevalent. Neurofeedback, a promising method, may become more sophisticated, allowing for precise interventions tailored to an individual's unique neurobiological profile.

Inclusive and Culturally Competent Practices

Recognizing the importance of cultural sensitivity in therapeutic practices will likely shape somatic therapy's future. Therapists are increasingly acknowledging that somatic healing is not a one-size-fits-all approach. Future trends in the field may see a greater emphasis on inclusive practices that consider cultural nuances, diverse belief systems, and varied expressions of trauma. Culturally competent somatic therapy seeks to create a space where individuals from all backgrounds feel seen, heard, and understood in the context of their unique cultural experiences.

Integrative Approaches: Collaboration with Other Healing Modalities

The future of somatic therapy may witness a greater integration with other holistic healing modalities. Collaborations with acupuncture, massage therapy, yoga, and mindfulness meditation can offer complementary approaches to somatic healing. Therapists may undergo cross-disciplinary training, allowing them to draw from diverse tools and techniques. This integrative approach acknowledges that somatic healing is part of a larger tapestry of well-being and recognizes the value of combining various modalities for comprehensive care.

Community-Centric Somatic Healing

Somatic therapy is expanding beyond the one-on-one therapeutic relationship to embrace community-based models. Group somatic therapy sessions, workshops, and community events may become more prevalent, fostering a sense of shared healing and mutual support. These community-centric approaches recognize the power of collective experiences in promoting resilience and post-traumatic growth. Additionally, online platforms may facilitate virtual communities, making somatic practices more accessible globally.

Environmental Somatics: Connecting Individuals to Nature

An emerging trend in somatic therapy is incorporating environmental elements into healing practices. Recognizing the profound impact of nature on well-being, therapists may explore eco-somatic approaches. Outdoor therapy sessions, nature retreats, and eco-therapy practices aim to reconnect individuals with the natural world, leveraging the therapeutic potential of the environment. This trend aligns with a broader cultural shift towards eco-consciousness and recognizing the interdependence between human and environmental health.

Embodied Creativity: Art and Expression in Somatic Healing

The intersection of somatic therapy and creative expression is a trend gaining momentum. Therapists recognize the power of artistic modalities such as dance, music, and visual arts in facilitating somatic exploration and healing. Future somatic therapy sessions may incorporate expressive arts therapies to tap into non-verbal modes of communication, providing individuals with alternative avenues for self-discovery and emotional expression. This approach recognizes the body as a canvas for creative exploration and healing.

Accessible and Inclusive Training Programs

As somatic therapy gains popularity, there is a growing need for accessible and inclusive training programs. Future trends may involve the development of online courses, workshops, and certification programs that make somatic therapy training more widely available. This democratization of knowledge aims to empower a diverse range of individuals, including those in underserved communities, to become somatic practitioners. Training programs also emphasize cultural competence, ensuring therapists are equipped to navigate the complexities of diverse healing journeys.

Research and Evidence-Based Practice

The future of somatic therapy will likely see an increased emphasis on rigorous research and evidence-based practice. As the field matures, there is a growing recognition of the need for empirical evidence to support the efficacy of somatic interventions. Research studies exploring the neurobiological mechanisms, long-term outcomes, and comparative effectiveness of somatic therapy approaches will contribute to the establishment of best practices and standards within the field.

Ethical Considerations and Professional Standards

With the evolving landscape of somatic therapy, ethical considerations and professional standards will become increasingly important. Future trends may involve the development of ethical guidelines specific to somatic practices, addressing issues such as informed consent for touch-based interventions, boundary management in body-centred work, and the responsible use of emerging technologies. Professional organizations may play a crucial role in establishing and upholding ethical standards to ensure clients' and practitioners' safety and well-being.

CONCLUSION

In the pursuit of holistic wellness, the integration of somatic therapy emerges as a pivotal cornerstone. Somatic therapy, with its roots deeply embedded in the intricate connection between the mind and the body, extends beyond traditional therapeutic approaches, offering a unique lens through which individuals can achieve profound well-being. As we traverse this therapeutic landscape, it becomes evident that somatic therapy is not merely a set of techniques but a philosophy that embraces the entirety of the human experience.

At its core, somatic therapy emphasizes the inseparable nature of physical sensations and emotional experiences. The intricate dance between the body and the mind becomes a focal point, acknowledging that our experiences, especially those rooted in trauma, are not confined to the cognitive realm alone. By recognizing and honouring the wisdom inherent in the body, somatic therapy contributes to a more comprehensive understanding of holistic wellness.

One of the central tenets of somatic therapy is the belief that the body is an archive of our lived experiences. It carries the imprints of joy, sorrow, love, and pain. This embodied history, often etched into our muscles and nervous system, can influence our well-being. Through its various techniques and modalities, somatic therapy seeks to unravel and heal these somatic imprints. As individuals engage in practices such as breathwork, movement, and mindfulness, they embark on a journey of self-discovery and release, allowing the body to shed the burdens it carries.

The therapeutic alliance formed in somatic therapy is a secure container for individuals to explore the depths of their embodied experiences. The therapist becomes a guide, helping clients navigate the terrain of their sensations and emotions. This collaborative process fosters a sense of safety and trust, essential elements for healing to unfold. As clients delve into the somatic realm, they often discover untapped reservoirs of resilience and strength, leading to a profound transformation in their overall well-being.

Furthermore, somatic therapy offers a nuanced approach to trauma recovery. Traumatic experiences, whether overt or subtle, can leave enduring imprints on the body and mind. Traditional therapeutic approaches may primarily focus on verbal expression, potentially bypassing the somatic aspects of trauma. Somatic therapy, on the other hand, provides a holistic avenue for processing and integrating traumatic memories. Through techniques such as sensorimotor psychotherapy and somatic experiencing, individuals can renegotiate their relationship with past trauma, fostering a sense of empowerment and resilience.

The implications of somatic therapy extend beyond the therapist's office into the fabric of daily life. Integrating somatic practices into one's routine becomes a transformative act of self-care. As individuals cultivate a heightened awareness of their bodies and sensations, they develop the tools to navigate life's challenges more easily. Mindful embodiment becomes a compass, guiding individuals through the complexities of their inner and outer worlds.

Moreover, the impact of somatic therapy on emotional regulation and resilience is noteworthy. The practices inherent in somatic therapy, such as grounding techniques and body scanning, equip individuals with skills to navigate emotional landscapes more effectively. By fostering a conscious connection with the body, individuals develop the capacity to regulate emotions in real time, reducing the likelihood of being overwhelmed by intense feelings. This enhanced emotional resilience becomes a beacon, illuminating the path towards a more balanced and centred existence.

Cultural and diversity considerations also play a crucial role in applying somatic therapy. Acknowledging diverse somatic experiences and cultural nuances is imperative for ensuring that somatic therapy is inclusive and accessible to individuals from various backgrounds. The intersectionality of identities, including but not limited to race, gender, and socio-economic status, must be woven into the fabric of somatic therapy practices to honour the richness of human diversity. As the field evolves, exploring ways to make somatic therapy culturally competent and responsive to everyone's unique needs is essential.

In contemplating the future of somatic therapy, it is evident that the field is on the cusp of continued innovation and growth. Research into the neurobiological underpinnings of somatic practices expands our understanding of how these interventions create lasting changes in the brain and body. Integrating technology, such as virtual reality and biofeedback, opens new avenues for delivering somatic interventions and expanding access to those in remote or underserved areas. The collaborative dialogue between somatic therapy and other therapeutic modalities, such as traditional talk therapy and expressive arts, holds promise for creating comprehensive and individualized treatment plans.

9 7 9 8 8 7 6 4 1 4 4 6 5